SLANKY

POEMS

MIKE DOUGHTY

SOFT SKULL PRESS
2002

SLANKY, ISBN: 1887128-71-9
ALL POEMS ©COPYRIGHT 1996 BY M. DOUGHTY.
ALL RIGHTS RESERVED.

EDITORIAL: TOM HOPKINS
COVER DESIGN: BENJAMEN PURVIS
ART DIRECTION: DAVID JANIK

FOR MORE INFORMATION ON MIKE DOUGHTY VISIT
WWW.SUPERSPECIALQUESTIONS.COM

PRINTED IN CANADA

SOFT SKULL PRESS, INC.
107 NORFOLK STREET
NEW YORK, NEW YORK 10002
WWW.SOFTSKULL.COM

DISTIRBUTED BY PUBLISHERS GROUP WEST
1.800.788.3123, WWW.PGW.COM

I'LL BE YOUR BABYDOLL, I'LL BE YOUR SEVEN-DAY FOOL

Tonight the train is a curveball
sloping towards portions of
Darkest Brooklyn; some house unlit,
like a blank face, where I assume
you sit unsatisfied in a cubical room.

IN THE MIND OF THE MIND

His mind is an angry place. When he is drunk, and can't explain himself, he says his mind is broken. Then he smacks his head repeatedly with the ball of his hand. Everybody laughs.

His mind is something that is very angry with him.

His mind is an angry sea of colors and references. His body bobs alone in it. His mind is an America for jingles and mottoes. Proud detergent names and happy cartoon animals with bow ties. They flock to him on ships. The labor on the assembly lines, screwing and drilling on the components of his dreams. They come out in the morning, smudged with soot.

His dreams are complex and ridiculous, Hong Kong epics of bullets and swords. Flying punches. Homely women in princess drag. Their reaching arms are draped with jewels. He slays her enemies but never screws her. His mind is indifferent to fucking. Though he pleads with it. A white arm emerges from behind the door and hangs a Do Not Disturb sign on the gilded knob. Every time. Then the credits roll, and his mind bills itself as best boy, electrician, cinematographer, gaffer, technician, Man In Hotel Lobby Number Two. Every time. Every time.

His mind is a jealous mind, always campaigning for his attention with garish colors and melodies. Waving its hands in front of his face to obscure the exterior influences. Even as those influences are welcomed inside and incorporated into the process of seduction.

And those influences that refuse the invitation become the object of murderous thoughts. Because the mind has only thoughts for hands, a murderous thought is in the mind the equal of murder. And the job becomes selling the pitch to its corporeal accomplice. But the sin is done.

Because the mind hates what is too big to swallow.

FOR CHARLOTTE, UNLISTED

Her room is still; a bed, a desk, and the one word Easy on typing paper taped to the wall. This is eight years later, still dreaming that room this night, alone, the hand drifting down—a gasp is gasped but the room still sits around me in its own July; the air there like walking underwater or through olive oil in a pan; the sheets quick to the skin like icing, her wide hips forcing my skinniness against the wall.

I fall to the carpet and drift off, the soul travelling to a nightclub behind a door deep in Sleeptown, and it's her, eight years later, same eyes and hands and everything, taking tickets.

The hour? I ask. How much? She gives the same answer as last time: No. There. No. More to the left. The back. Anywhere. Again. Please.

ROOTLESS

We roamed across Texas in a rented car,
buzzing with aimlessness, squinting
in the dull, hard light.
The greenery shooting past us slowly hardened,
turning into desert, burning away like a menthol into space.
We stopped on a gravel flatland
to piss and smoke, wandering off
to the powerlines at the edges
of our eyes' grasp. Onward.

By the junction, up on the panhandle,
you slept, mumbling a pulp of words
to an unseen companion.
The air curling out of your nose,
droning into your mouth
like a kiss reversed on itself.
Your eyes flashed open and threw down
a bleary glance at the white dashes
and shut again. I could smell you.
My head bent, straining through the whoosh,
to listen. The baby words fell from your lips,
and I sifted them for music,
trying to hear the meaning
in a sucking sound.

OTHER FISH

A girl with a backpack on a cellular phone sighs;
between the exhale and the first consonant
a van barrels through her. And who knows
what the boy thinks, his line slipping from her voice,
her words sucked backwards through the wire?
Two hours from now he'll be drunk,
his slurred thoughts slobbering over motives,
why she decided suddenly to leave him
and hung up mid-word.

The phone yelps angrily from under a bus,
and she lays splayed like an asterisk
in the dreary sentence of Fourteenth Street.

FROM A GAS STATION OUTSIDE PROVIDENCE

This kiss, unfinished,
lips to receiver in the parking lot,
a pucker shot through a fiber optic wire
to an answering machine
toward switchboards and stations transmitting
in blips to satellites, this kiss
thrown earthward and shooting down
coils, around pipeline and electric power
lumbering underground,
up threads and transistors
and transference points.

This kiss is zeroes and ones jumbled
and tossed into a pneumatic system,
unscrambled at the end and scrawled
onto a tape recorder slowly rolling
at the side of your bed,
then slapping back, reverbed
off the ringer, a tinny phantom
of the smooch like a smack on
an aluminum can, up the same
veins through the belly of the same satellite
and softly to the side of my head;
this kiss is home before the next exhalation leaves.

I'm stooped in the booth,
pounding quarters into the slot;
yellow light droops over the asphalt,
and your ghost, too cool
and elusive with those hands and mouth
sings around me in the smell of gasoline;
whose mouth is this, scratched in static,
some droplet of a sigh, atomized,
and sputtering digitized into my room?

NERVE INJECTIONS

A man has premonitions of his teeth cracking every time he looks at concrete. Like the converse of an amputee's ghost pain, he can't feel it but his mouth acts as if he can. He feels his teeth as one solid plate, his mouth dammed with china. He becomes so sick of his teeth screaming that he goes to an unlicensed dentist in a seedy quarter and is injected in his mouth with painkillers to numb them. He becomes an addict but denies this to himself and walks around pillowed from the world.

Later, he freefalls on ice. He carries his teeth home in his wallet. He reassembles the cracked ones with tile epoxy on the kitchen table. He puts them in the icetray in his freezer. For the rest of his life a slathering junkie, he gums hard candy unaware that splinters of jawbreaker are slitting gashes in the sockets in his jaw.

SOUND AGAINST THE EQUAL SIGN

Behind wire frames, a mind narrows like a splinter of light through a magnifying glass and onto a withering ant. All arithmetic predicates itself on a notion of balance; wild growths of equations differ like species of birds, but even that disharmony is made similar as taxpayers by the equal sign. Those parallel lines; a thin mouth, expressionless. He's easy with the split of his worlds; the illogic that runs through the brains of people he buys milk from is shadowed by a world in which a shape will transpose itself, with a shrug, into a hypoteneuse.

In a clarinet, there is no sense. In a swell of brass, there is no balance. Music is the weird cousin of math; the symbols grow unchecked, without an equational mirror to justify them. No other desire is so maddening; to drool over a pear placed seductively on a table manifests a physiological need. To let his eyes wander to a pair of thighs manifests a genetic imperative. Sound is the perception of a wave created by the movement of object against object against air. Harmony is the manifestation of a tone above another tone. Hearing a confection of violins, he shakes off his pleasure angrily; all numbers have names and surnames of exponentials and zeroes, but the notes lurk everywhere as faces with nothing but eyes.

His mind defeats itself in attempting to quantify this; all sound carries a logical tonality, he thinks, and trains himself to notice this. The clack of a heel on a staircase produces a matter-of-fact D sharp. Carhorns harmonize with dialtones in a droning G. The notes of all things waver not only on the absolute tones, but on a million points between them, dividing and subdividing in a random, infinite slash into the flesh of the mathematical world.

Sitting sullenly at his desk, spinning a pencil, he suddenly hears a doorbell collide with a cough over the subsonic hum of a television, and leaps up with joy. His face drops. He is lost.

PORTRAITS IN SHOW BUSINESS NUMBER ONE

On the street they come up to Fran Tarkenton and tell him about their disappointments, their failures, their dead marriages. They want a brass cure, accomplished and shiny like a Heisman trophy. They tell him, Fran Tarkenton, we're hurting, you're an award-winning broadcaster and former All-American, come back to our life and save us. But Fran Tarkenton cannot help them, and he goes to sleep in hotel rooms on his lecture tours and is troubled by the hell of the lives of the people.

Fran Tarkenton goes to the President, who is his friend, and tells him that the marriages of the people have died. The President goes to the television station and tells knock-knock jokes on the air. He tells them to get together and love one another. The people, who elected him, are soothed.

The FBI has Fran Tarkenton killed, on television, and blames it on the President and a man who they happened to employ as a bicycle messenger nine years ago, and who happened to have a shotgun on him that day when he went to his job at the television station. Because he was going to shoot his wife. The FBI does not want the people to get together and love one another.

PORTRAITS IN SHOW BUSINESS NUMBER TWO

Joe Franklin was known to ply his guests with bottled water, extravagant because he bought it and it tastes like nothing. He wore an indigo dress. The lovable Marky Mark was there. His drummer was in the midst of a painful divorce, and the cameraman fell down repeatedly but always got up in time. They sang "Mr. Funny Man." Seven angels slew the beast Joe Franklin sat upon behind the desk and cut off his arms, which had become snakes and spat poison spit on Victor Borge. Victor Borge, who had found Jesus that afternoon on an exit ramp, instantly vanished and was in heaven.

PORTRAITS IN SHOW BUSINESS NUMBER THREE

Cookie Monster, burnt out and hateful of children, concocts a suicide plot under the auspices of televised entertainment; stripped and chained up, he is lifted into a velvet sack, placed in a steamer trunk full of holes so as to sink faster, sealed, and thrown into a lake before throngs. The band plays, and in the sealed trunk, in the velvet sack, Cookie Monster waits to drown.

WHEN I WAS SMALL

When I was small, when I was very small, I would lay by the television and dream of the apocalypse. I would dream of the power of the Hydrogen Bomb. I dreamed my world engulfed in a divine and furious fire. I hoped for it.

WHEN I SAW IT

It was in the garden. I went there, and I looked. And when I saw it, I could not help but to desire it.

I had to pull back the branches to see it. It was late, and the forms of the branches were cast dark against the dark blue sky. There was light, but it huddled to the side of the house. The light flickered over it, randomly, in moments, peekabooing its mysteries. I pulled back the branches, and I looked.

Its sound was like breathing sounds underwater. I could barely hear the sound. And there was a hissing in the air. So I had to strain. I had to tilt my head and push my ear to it.

After this, I would always strain to listen. It was meaningless to look. I met a woman once and told her about this. But she would get angry when I didn't look at her when I spoke. When she spoke, I would push my ear toward her, and she would grab my chin and pull my face to face her. She would think I wasn't listening when I wasn't looking. I left her, but sneakily, just quietly withdrawing myself from her life. She is still angry about that.

She made an amazing sound. I don't know how she made it. I don't remember what the sound sounded like, but I remember the way it filled me. And she had a smell that my mind convinced me was not perfume, but her. I don't remember what the smell smelled like, but I remember the way it filled me. Unlike the sound, though, I am reminded of it when that perfume passes by on other women.

I thought she was the answer. She was not the answer. I have continued to look for the answer, but I have not found it. Instead, I have gained an astounding skill in locating flaws. The answer was simple once, the way math looks in childhood, two digits and a symbol. The answer is a beast now, with tangents and greek numerals, cubed and multiplied. Its algebra has grown unchecked.

It was in the garden. I went there, and I looked. And when I saw it, I could not help myself but to desire it.

I could tell you about the first time I kissed her, which was so compelling it shot me with fright. I could tell you about the first time I saw the way the bone of her hip curves from the side. Lust is ugly like this, this kind of lust where you keep making phonecalls and phonecalls, anxious to see if her voice still exists. Where she becomes mildly creeped when you stare while she reads her book. And she lashes back with vengeful amorousness, such that the sex ceases to be sex, and becomes a brawl of each prying the other open.

Thousands of months have passed since that time. She continues to call me. She says I am unlike anyone else she has ever slept with, in that she continues to call me. She told me about them all. She told me about the one that got her pregnant, and how after that whatever was between them died, and how she believes that as a species in context we are here to yield replacements, and that when this fails, the mind starts chasing other options, elsewhere. She told me about the woman she slept with, who was a minor friend in school. For weeks after she was saddened by the subtle incongruities between those who mostly love those who are like them and those who mostly love those who are unlike them. She told me about the boy she fucked on a boat in the Gulf of Mexico.

She has their phone numbers on scraps in a desk drawer. I've seen them spilling out when she opens it.

So when she called me, I went back there, to her house. And when I got there, she was on the phone. But her hand moved across me while she talked on the phone. And she hung up the phone, and we stumbled backwards, upstairs, kissing, up to the bed. And we were all but fucking before we fell on to it.

It was in the garden. I went there, and I looked. And when I saw it, I could not help myself but to desire it.

MY LOVER LIVES ON THE OTHER COAST

I do what
my baby bids
me do;

across this side-effect of manifest destiny

I fly
to you.

ALL THIS FROM TWO EYES TWITCHING

Some sallow accountant of dreams
has spilt pop on the margin
of the legder of your memory,
blurred the ink itemizing
this object and that individual
now starring as Loss or Indecision
in tonight's cinematic rendering
of current events.

Now the whole business is ruined
with sweetness and blended irreparably;
the landscape is caked with sugar,
the plot is a saccharine mess,
and as you fuck some neutral hybrid
of your mother and a boy from the sixth grade,
your mouth purses from a sickly honey taste.

Your nightmares have gone to cheery filmic convention.

When the alarm clock invades,
it's a blast from the trumpets
of the heroes, on white horses,
returned to slay the monster chasing you.

INSOMNIA

My love and my sleep
light their smokes off
the kitchen stove,
sucking at the blue fire
on the grill.
They stare each other down
with dull eyes
kissing glances
eye tag
look-and-lookaway
while
through the next room's wall
my body sprawls
like a colossus prone
on a bed and blankets landscape
I'm hearing shuffling,
pace, return, shuffling,
fingers drumming
on the counter, a tattoo
drumming up soldiers
to formation.

When morning slips the bolt
off the lock and slides
into the living room easy
I will empty the ashtrays
and receive the fruit of
their negotiations
then sleep the day dry
with their alignment pact
on the bedside table.

This is my song in lieu of dreams,
four a.m., no matches, no coffee, quarter moon.

PETER MACK

They hooked some massive weight
to the underside of his jaw
and left it there for his formative years,
stretching it cartoonish, grim,
and disquietingly long, and left him,
fluvial in his suit and tie
to wade through the world
with a frown concave in that
astounding chin, muttering
in singsong: Whaaaaat?

A MIAMI FOR THE TALK SHOW HOSTS

They built a city out of raw stucco in the swamps by the ocean for the talk show hosts to go die in. Creaking, still in the blue suits from wardrobe that they wore to entertain America from cue cards. Now, playing chess at their very own desks with special imaginary guests and broken microphones installed by the management as a concession to their paranoid demands, they all talk like mad sportswriters and go all fuzzy in the subtropical heat, looking back bitterly on careers as sleeping aids. They've all gone to conspiracy theories that grew on them like a mold, they all check their meals in the cafeteria for poision and are alert for the ruses of the dreaded network police.

A barren, violent place, there have been stabbings over arguments of who knew Liza best. "Is this aberration how we reward those who have served their country well?" one was heard asking moments before another lunged at him with a pencil. "Look in my wallet, here, these are my grandchildren and my demographics; a couple more points I woulda been in Malibu with Dick Van Dyke, not here festering with a mutt like you."

JUNGLE OF NUMBERS

a deck of cards

1.
In the mind of my mind,
a hand sauters
motives to coils.

2.
He embraced his lawyer.

3.
Geography pulls no magic on me,
today.

4.
In transit, pursued
by his managers.

5.
Over like it never was and
exhausted like a dead man
he looked down and knew
the red in her mouth.

6.
Who was the Egypt's Pharaoh of
the Honkytonk Blues?

7.
Shoulders pushed back,
it leans toward the daylight
and into the eye of noon.

8.
The Sultan

9.
The Magnate

10.
The Inscrutable Deejay McMonkey

11.
The Prime Dog

12.
Everybody needs a hook;
my hook is the fez.

13.
Here Comes the Bliss Boy

14.
Swank

15.
Lies

16.
The Hand of the Unknown

17.
The Hand of Unseen Sequence

18.
The Hand of Randomness

19.
The Hand of Unspeakable
Languages

20.
The Calculating Engine

21.

You're the kind of girl that would
break up Van Halen

22.

Herbal Mama?
Herbal Mama.

23.

Elliot Groffman, attorney-at-law,
riding elephants
in the mountains
of Thailand.

24.

He counted in his head,
drifting, as the radiator cooed.

25.

I hope you get there.
I hope you enjoy yourself.

26.

Cruel and unusual.

27.

As the band laughed,
her finger traced his spine,
and he folded into her.

28.

B is for bird, who bit a boy and
tore his eyes out. For breaking all
his toys.

29.

The spiny creatures of the deep

30.

Under your pillow, the gun
breathes.

31.

Shackled with contractual
obligations.

32.

Superstars of the Hong Kong
Cinema!

33.

No toy duck, firetruck!

34.

Pulling gears
to hear the switches click;
feeling a gust of nerves.

35.

An organ chord,
chintzy, rippling,
wavering towards Venus.

36.

Randall Davis Kaye
could not dance
to any kind
of music.

37.

All is Lost

38.
The runt of all numbers;
the number of all runts

39.
Milk and Cigarettes

40.
Sin Will Find You Out

41.
In the lobby,
thousands
of regal women from
accounting,
their hair in smart slants,
heels stinging the floor
like a rain of cutlery
drumming on the Parthenon

42.
All hopped up on goofballs

43.
Far off,
above the Flatbush Extension,
a plane scraped its belly
across a sooty yellow moon.

44.
She found her bliss between the
headphones, and pursed her lips.

45.
Do you have any dolls that can
walk or talk?

46.
Her white neck. By the open door.

47.
She had a long nose, and curves as
sharp as the letter 'X'.

48.
He watched the bodies, fluid in the
lagoon.

49.
Shoveling coal into the open grate.

50.
Driving under a tangle of overpass-
es.

51.
She watches the record spin,
pained by surfacing dreams
of bourbon and cigarettes

52.
I'll saw those suckers down.

53.
But sleep won't come.

54.
Texas vs. France, who wins?

HERE COMES THE PANIC NOW

What do the dogs know?
On Camrose, in a jumble of lots,
the barking came through stucco
with flowers cut into the wall.

What tremor comes, unheard,
gathering its roll now in the hills,
to rush in and sway the palm trees,
skinny and dour?

LOW IMPEDANCE

I stutter these things out to you
like drunk men hazard
Mingus records,
stumbling liquored over
time changes and bursts.
Like sane men let
those records jitter them
into submission—kinetic,
spat out, and it throws itself
clattering downhill. Christ.
This is me snapping
piano wires with my
fingernails, struggling
toward some unknown
lustrous chord, plunking
the bass cables and slapping at
the long spread of upper octaves.

Now at a payphone
in a stinging wind,
she calls this random corner
and, huddling in a clamshell booth,
my voice hoarses out to her,
clicking like a card on
bicycle spokes. I mutter,
I can't fight the law of averages,
and slam the receiver down,
the ringer sending
a loony note
pinging like blame
down Fulton Street,
toward Borough Hall.

LUTHER MISSED

Once, staring into the eye of a revolver,
he cried out, swearing to a life of holiness.

The gun stuck, and the gunman shrugged.

He lived out the next twelve years in a motel
in Indiantown, watching movies on the television
inside the powder blue walls, ignoring the oath,
which followed him in the eyes of night clerks
sweeping the lobby.

TRUE STORY OF THE PEOPLE HAD OVER

It was late August, in the week before
she tore off to Kansas, Colorado, and the Deep South
with my conga player—my conguero I liked
to call him, who had lent me a beautiful hat
and never asked for its return,
I don't mean this to highlight
my unburdened opinion of him, I mean
drummers are built for betrayal this
friend of mine Teresa says she fucks
them 'cause they're half the ego twice
the stamina—she called and said
she was Having People Over,
some unspecified Bon Voyage,
I remember how dumb the words sounded.
I declined. The next day when she was
gone with my conguero I drove past
Tenth Street where she lived, in this
obsessive need to spy on her roommates,
snubbing the dope vendors on their stoop.

The day they came back, I drove past
the Port Authority in the hope she and my
conguero would be happening out of the gates
and I would take them into my van, weary
and spent in each others' arms,
drive them until they fell asleep and then
abandon them at the mouth of the
Lincoln Tunnel in Hoboken. Is it Hoboken?
But no. Later when I saw her she told me
she missed me and asked if I missed her
and I said no, so she asked me again
until I lied and said yes and she won.

MISS AUDREY

A man studded like a scepter on the roadside and dusted with asphalt walks
into a mansion and finds two men with money playing ping-pong. Two men
with sheet music in their bank vaults, offices downtown near the Opera
House, secretaries. They act glad to see him but they keep playing ping-pong,
and I say, so would you like to hear him sing? And they say yes, why don't
you sing?

Nashville under low clouds, chintz everywhere and good clean money and
fun. Mansions on the edge, Homes-of-the-Stars. Radio towers blinking; deep in
their waves sings the high lonesome sound. If a giant man came out of the
Atlantic Ocean and walked across the lower forty-eight, the city would go
like a tack into the ball of his foot. Too much blood and beer. Everybody's
too happy to look drunk. Everybody owns an automobile. Everybody dresses
like themself, back wherever they're from they stood out like sequins on a
rubber raincoat, here everybody looks like this with big notes and treble
clefs, cacti, guitars sewn into the fabric.

And the steel guitars go: Wheeeeeee. High lonesome.

Anyhow they made him a star that afternoon. That's the kind of men that
walk around Nashville. Except it wasn't that quick, there was some kind of
papers to sign. They had to dust him off. They bought him a song from a
dumb Jew with a piano in New York. Fake sentiment, but it's all fake in terms
of the songs, it's singers that are real. This is true whether the song comes
from someplace real or not. He sang it and these powerful powerful men put
it on vinyl and walked it over to a radio station, and then another, and then
another. It only takes an afternoon. It only takes an afternoon.

No. That's a lie.

You want to know where the money is? I tell you. There was a scrapyard
outside of town, it was on a clay flat. They could not put a building there
because it would sink. They burrowed into the heaps of scrap and came up
with the clay. Which they built his body out of and breathed song into. They
named him the Hillbilly Golem. That's the whole process. They didn't have to
make him a star because they acted like he was a star and nobody wanted to
contradict them. They bought the records because

they felt obligated, and then were seduced by it. Nobody ever got sad before that. That record ruined everything in everybody's life. Then they invented drink, and we were all hopeless.

It was the suit, not the body. You could hear the gleam on the radio. Like a halo around the sound of the record. The surface noise once the record gets real old. This was the kind of fabric that makes you want to moan out loud on the municpal bus. Blinding fabric, relentless fabric like how a lawyer makes men break down under oath. Under all the weight of all the words of their lives. It was merciless, yes. And he did regret it, yes. He never meant to hurt anybody. He said to me once, he said, Audrey, the methods of the revolution become the methods of the regime. But the killing went on. I remember the bodies that littered the streets of Nashville. We knew all of their names, once. You forgot them. I remember the charts. I remember the competition. I am the only one that remembers them now. Roy Acuff, found cut up, parts of Fred Rose spread around somebody's garden. Moon Mullican, ran through with a guitar neck. Cutesy Kitty Wells, the cunt, choked. Kill or be killed, that's the law of the hillbilly music industry.

Sometimes it seems like I'm sorry for it, now.

OUTLYING SEATTLE

Utsaladdy
Burien
Puyallup
Rosehilla
Suquamish
Portage
Issaquah
McMurray
Snoqualmie
Spanaway
Carbonado
Yelm
McKenna
Tulalip
Tumwater
Kapowsin
Tenino
Port Gamble
Monroe
Juanita
Navy Yard City
Magnolia Beach
Olalla
Lofall
Elgin
Enumclaw
Buckley
Black Diamond
Centralia
Chehalis
Steilacoom
Hadlock
Chimacum
Warm Beach
Silvana
View Park
Tukwila

BUTTER / LOST

Against hands, a smooth
is smoothed around
and skin
rushed up to it,
cooing sweat like a whistle
defecting a steampipe.

Oiled, the machine chuffs,
and the brain is dry, and the nerves
scurry off with messages to no one
in charge, while this equals this;
two arms locked into each other
are without a mind to differentiate
between limbs and hips, therefore,
I have come here to get lost.

THE INCREDIBLE MAGNETIC MAN

Onward to Victory, mule,
with a subatomic glimmer of rage
humming a hot inch below the cheekbones

moving down Water Street like an ox
bound in fleshy lumber, muscles and lumps
punched up and numb like insect bites

Inside the contours of veins blown up
by mosquitos into thick balloons,
a single radiowave transmits itself
into loose bits of metal scattered around;
Keys. Beltbuckles. Scissors. Headphones.

Streetlights sizzle like bees being taken to slaughter.

On Water Street, two legs
are the clack of drills
spearing into the blacktop

in the light further down
what you can only hope will be
some Imperial China is actually
the orange noise
at the ends of cigarettes
glowing at your approach

THE BUG WRANGLER

He was jailed for cruelty to insects, and his agent wasn't answering the phone, so he stayed awake in the cell all night, pictures jumping around his head of the cops and the blowdryer they took as evidence. He used the blowdryer to force the spiders to move, up the arm of a stuntwoman, across a floor. He was known to the industry as a professional, that he could coax wrenching performances from the crankiest bugs. He was a man famed for producing bug performances that would make people weep in the theaters.

They knew what they were jumping into, he thought, I always split the money square, am I wrong? You take some roach out of a miserable life and put it in pictures. Tame the wildest insects with a flashlight and a little blowdryer technology. Go to the beasts and teach them respect. Take them into your home and live with them. They betray you to the police for giving them this.

At a press conference, he sat at the microphone with a loyal spider whom he tried to coax a positive character statement out of, but he couldn't use the blowdryer in front of the media, and the spider stood there and said nothing while he sweated and the videotape rolled on forward.

SHE GOT THE GOOD SHOES, SHE GOT THE BAD TEETH

In a dim bar, the treble rose
in sharpness around her.

The frequencies went straight to the teeth.

She was meringue
in a green suit, her silver
shoes radiating,
and a shimmy that sent
her hips in a liquid
piston motion to the floor
like cream shifting in a glass.
One glance; the eye on the eye
sizzled like crayons
on super 8 film,
and she bared
angry monkey teeth at me—
each tooth its own moon
in a pollution town,
tobacco-stained pickups
on a junkstore guitar.

BICOASTAL

Each city is its own dream life.
In each, the other the dream.
He is awake only on airplanes.
He hurdles weeks
through the calendar
in each city,
longing for the other.

BY THE LIGHT OF THE SILVERY SILVERY

Goodnight, mud by the thousands
of whatever unit they measure mud by;
you can't move through it without missing
the angry bleached light
of usual. A bubble of humidity
forms above everything, and is
scratched open by the frictions of
machines moving
and human energies.

Hope dies and I
shake off the excess water,
spend a half hour crafting some opening
statement, but only give her my coat
and say It's a gift. For me, she says,
eyeballs floating to the top of the eye,
and I can't speak, but hand-signal: Victory.

BRECHT SAID FASCISM IS NOT THE OPPOSITE OF DEMOCRACY BUT A DISTORTION OF IT IN A TIME OF CRISIS

A boy bought an ant farm, ants, x-ray glasses, and absolute power with nothing but proofs of purchase. He ordered them from an ad in a comic book.

He bred the ants and raised an army, and those the ants could not eat he would drive away, whimpering, by wearing the glasses and telling them in a calm but sinister voice that he could see their underwear. He conquered his own world and never had to go to sleep again. His parents came to him for mercy from the ants, but were tried and hung.

One night he collapsed after watching television without pause for two weeks. The ants, bored of destroying the lamp fixtures and wrecking the furniture, stole the glasses from his unconscious face and chased him, screaming, around the house, looking without pity upon his underwear. They ambushed him in the shower, where he hid because he felt safe behind the distorted-glass door, and ate him whole, and then were bored again.

KETOSIS

That love that burns your muscles down from inside is known by the medical term Ketosis. This is the product of Anorexia. This is when the body, starved for other food, exploits other tissues for warmth. For strength. Your body consumes itself. This is where you are. You are now an onion with a spark inside it. Here I am, trying to peel each layer off, toward the essential truth in the center. Meanwhile, the center is burning outward, to reach my hand. That is, I hope it burns to meet my hand.

I do not know if you love me, or if you love your own skinniness. I love your skinniness. I love the whole of your self. I love the way you curve, and the bone under that, and whatever it is under that that moves around under my hand when my hand is on you. When my hand is on you, I can feel two things twitching—the liquid movement of your spirit from side to side, and a faint buzz, some kind of gnawing. Two loves in tandem, moving to two separate ambitions.

I do not think the love of your skinniness is the same thing as your love for me.

This is what I do—I go to a storefront, where I buy a small bag. The bag is made of wax paper. Inside the wax paper is a small amount of cocaine. Then I go back to the apartment, where you are. I pour the cocaine onto the table, and I snort some, and sometimes you snort some. You usually don't. And then, when that elated feeling starts to overwhelm me, my mind is full. And then I cease to be hungry for anything, except to fuck you, and except for my own selfish fascinations with what is moving around in my own mind. And then I feel like I'm actually with you.

Cocaine is interesting as a drug, because most drugs do two things; One, they make you feel a good feeling, and B, they make you want to have more. Cocaine is the reverse of this. There is a good hour with cocaine, where you chatter and jump around and a thousand things connect in your mind and become whole and logical. But, mostly, the moment it enters your nose you are compelled to snort more. After that hour, the feeling becomes incidental. The feeling is a side effect in a blur of consumption for its own sake.

In that hour, we fuck on the couch, and then we fuck in the bed. And after, both gaunt bodies stay locked, trembling a little from the shock of release and all the burning going on inside them. And then, locked to you, I start to babble and babble. Something about the drug allows me to talk without caring if you hear me or not. Because you look absorbed. You're elsewhere. Every part of you is concentrated on some inner point where you're choosing some muscle to burn, some nerve to throw on the fire. Every part of your conscious mind is tracing the inside shell of the onion, looking for specks of fuel. My body unlocks and begins to search the outside world for more.

So I leave, and when I'm at the door, I say; Do you want anything? And you say; No. Nothing. And I say; Are you sure. And you say; No. Nothing.

And I go, and then I'm back, with more. You're on the same couch. You're still naked, maybe with a shirt thrown loose on your skinny shoulders, or a blanket wrapped around the grill of your ribs. Your eyes are still focused somewhere else. Maybe you do a little, and the spark in the onion eases up on the inner layers and burns the cocaine for awhile. Or maybe you smoke a cigarette, and the spark laps at the fumes. But your body becomes exhausted, and you fall asleep, askew on the cushions.

I am awake for hours, spastic, walking around the room, one eye watching you sleep. You don't look like you're dreaming at all. When I lay down, I try not to move. Though everything about me is astutter, I try not to startle you awake. I sleep, eventually.

In the morning, I make coffee before you're awake. I am for some reason compelled to stumble out of the bed at an insanely early hour, my head stuck up with thickness, my muscles slack and useless. When you rise, we drink the coffee, yours with milk. My body consoles itself with the minor stimulant. And, in yours, somewhere in the center, the spark licks at the trickle of nourishment.

BEDSPINS

Drunk, she was carried
and thrown into the pillows.
She stamped her foot on the floor
as she slept, to keep the world
from spinning away from her
like a troubled childhood.

DESCENT OF TOOLS

Iron chunks fight upward
to the surface of the world;

The simple ax
was made to make
the candlestick
was made to make
the blunderbuss
was made to make
the lock, moveable type
was made to make
the steam engine
was made to make
the outboard motor, the toaster, the transistor,
was made to make
the speaker that sings to you
while we speak, now.

Your only instinct is convenience,
and the hand of your convenience
moves to build a mind
superior to yours.

LONG GONE FROM VAUDEVILLE

The infamous comedian in
business class pauses
lips over plastic;
the liquid whooshes down
with pills between tight
nervous breaths; he lets
the throat relax; sleep.
Four hours pass.
At the carousel in a stupor,
pawing through autographs.

THE BOY IS A FRAUD

You can be
anything
as long
as you got
the shoes
to prove it;
as long as you got
the walk down;
as long as you don't
flinch

This can be
all you
for real
you can go
all these places
for real

You can say
this belongs to you
for real
you can clutch
your reference books
and conjure
the fine words out
with your fine thin fingers
small and
circling above
the pages
stirring up
allies
in your defense
against language
as a thing
which is
not pretty
but actually
speaks.

You want proof
that you are
what the shoes
connote;
not clean thoughts
but lush music
and you
lie awake
sweating
wondering where you
bought the myth
wondering how much
it costs
to make your pain
valid.

WHOSE MUSIC?

He lives in absolute terror of a saxophone he has kept under his bed for four years. He played it since his mouth learned to blow, then put it under the bed four years ago because he had grown bored of it and moved on to affairs with lovelier instruments; a clarinet for two months, a flute for awhile, the drums. He went back to the saxophone and couldn't face it unashamed, so he put it under the bed and learned to play sociology, the jewel of all musical instruments. This all had something to do with the difference between fingerpainting and Jackson Pollock, or Motherwell, or when a man plays stupid noise he finds attractive on a violin he can't play, as opposed to the man who can play études but chooses to screech. The joy, the redemptive power of the horn he felt unentitled to, as if he had to pay more to get his interest back from the saxophone.

Now he fears the saxophone will end up in his mouth like a crackpipe, that twenty years from now he will look back on that one delirious hour with the reed in his mouth, his fingers tapping the brass, and regret it forever. That he will end up some sham Anthony Braxton, always in fear that people will discover him as a fraud. Or that he would spend the rest of his life like Anthony Braxton, scribbling pictures of bicycles and numbers to describe tunes that, language having been stolen from him by the music, he can't name.

Yesterday he remembered his affair with the clarinet, momentarily on the D train, over the Manhattan Bridge, and was momentarily swept upward by the memory of the clarinet's wood smell. This somehow coupled with the scenery, the blue riveted-iron bridge that colored his memory like a drink mixed with mathematics and Duke Ellington.

HERE'S HOW IT ENDS

Here's how it ends: he gets the girl. He gets the money. His loyal sidekick
jumps up from behind the rock and shouts Hey! distracting the firing squad.
The sidekick is cut down, but the girl and he escape through the treacher-
ous badlands, and the sidekick ascends to Glory in an orchestra of senti-
ment. Around the vicious curve, his car skids by sideways, on two wheels,
while the enemy careens over a cliff and is tumbling, tumbling, tumbling, and
explodes! In a fight, he knocks the enemy off the scaffolding and leaps into
the water before the gas tank explodes! He parachutes into the green moun-
tains before the smoking plane explodes! She fears him drowned, but he
emerges from the sea! The mysterious sheik removes his veil and is not the
sheik at all, but the sidekick, not dead! The sidekick is not dead at all! The
girl is not dead at all! The palace is on fire but the king alive! The oil tanker
is sunk but the lovable captain alive! The rocket is wrecked but the robot
walks! The Cadillac is swallowed by the quicksand, but the happy pimp with
the heart of gold laughs, though the briefcase full of money sinks with it, in the
trunk! Why? Because the money is counterfeit!

The detective slays the monster! The explorer defeats the mad scientist! The
boy defeats the alien! The average man conquers the forces of darkness! And
then he is with the girl.

And then he is with the girl.
And then he is with the girl.
And then he receives his rich reward.
And then he kisses the girl.
And then the sun goes down.
In the life raft.
On the shore.
In the plucky little town.
On the frozen tundra.
In the speeding convertible.
In the posh watering holes of Glittering Manhattan.
In the lush jungle.
On the dock.
In glamourous Monte Carlo.
In mysterious old Baghdad.
In the desert.

In the forest.
In the hills.
On the courthouse steps.

In the center of the sea.

TRANSATLANTIC

Only sex and flight lost time like this.
Pop songs are curves of the same length,
outside the sight of the clock.
In this plane,
above this ocean,
my headphones swell with
bitter melodies
candied in echoplex
and fattened violins,
cooed at by low thrums
that reshape themselves
into your open mouth,
your hips slithering around me.
There is a tiny gap in my mind,
where the moan you made sat.
I only remember how it felt to hear it.
It comes back to me like a song I heard and loved,
but that dissipated, leaving
a phantom trace of notes in sequence
that probably doesn't exist. I can hear
the breath around it, though,
and as the plane jitters through turbulence,
as the melody, cupped to the sides of my head
like your hands did slants
toward a lush and glorious crash
of cymbals and chords, your tongue stirs
a weird magic into the mix.
Outside the window of the plane,
there is nothing,
and under that,
water and water and water.